W9-CSL-819

VANCOUVER *Flashbacks*

Selected by Anne Norman

A Firefly Postcard Book

A FIREFLY BOOK

Firefly Books Ltd.
250 Sparks Ave.
Willowdale, Ontario M2H 2S4

Copyright © 1990 Firefly Books Ltd.

ISBN 0-920668-64-X

Design: DUO Strategy and Design Inc.
Picture selection and captions: Anne Norman
Printed in Canada

Photographs courtesy Vancouver Public Library

VANCOUVER

In this little book you will find Vancouver the way it looked to residents and tourists through the last century. Many of the landmarks have vanished and streetscapes have changed, but this is a nostalgic reminder of the way Vancouver developed.

Thanks to the Vancouver Public Library for access to its excellent photographic archive.

VANCOUVER *Flashbacks*

English Bay with the old bathhouse, c. 1906.

Firefly Books Ltd., 250 Sparks Ave., Willowdale, Ontario M2H 2S4

Permission of Vancouver Public Library

VANCOUVER *Flashbacks*

Looking west on Hastings from Homer, 1910. The
banners reveal the spirit of boosterism as the city
rapidly grew as a port, trading centre and financial
headquarters for the booming resource industries.

Firefly Books Ltd., 250 Sparks Ave., Willowdale, Ontario M2H 2S4

Permission of Vancouver Public Library

VANCOUVER *Flashbacks*

Second Beach in Stanley Park, early 1900s. In 1888, the federal government granted a 400-hectare military reserve to the city as a public park, named for the Governor General, Lord Stanley.

Firefly Books Ltd., 250 Sparks Ave., Willowdale, Ontario M2H 2S4

Permission of Vancouver Public Library

VANCOUVER *Flashbacks*

White Lunch restaurant, c. 1916.

Firefly Books Ltd., 250 Sparks Ave., Willowdale, Ontario M2H 2S4

Permission of Vancouver Public Library

VANCOUVER *Flashbacks*

City Market on the south side of False Creek, 1908.
Vancouver's electric streetcar service began in 1890
and expanded throughout the city.

Firefly Books Ltd., 250 Sparks Ave., Willowdale, Ontario M2H 2S4

Permission of Vancouver Public Library

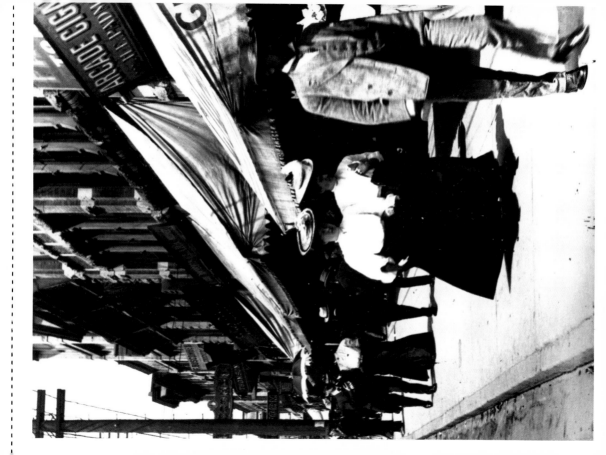

VANCOUVER *Flashbacks*

North side of Hastings, looking west from Hamilton,
early 1900s.

Firefly Books Ltd., 250 Sparks Ave., Willowdale, Ontario M2H 2S4

Permission of Vancouver Public Library

VANCOUVER *Flashbacks*

Automobile being rescued by a horse during a car
rally in Burnaby, early 1900s.

Firefly Books Ltd., 250 Sparks Ave., Willowdale, Ontario M2H 2S4

Permission of Vancouver Public Library

VANCOUVER *Flashbacks*

Looking west on Hastings from near Granville, c. 1910.
The old post office building with its clock tower has
been renovated inside with shops and restaurants.

Firefly Books Ltd., 250 Sparks Ave., Willowdale, Ontario M2H 2S4

Permission of Vancouver Public Library

VANCOUVER *Flashbacks*

Shaughnessy Service Station, Granville at 14th, 1927.

Firefly Books Ltd., 250 Sparks Ave., Willowdale, Ontario M2H 2S4

Permission of Vancouver Public Library

VANCOUVER *Flashbacks*

Looking south on Granville from Hastings, 1908. The
Williams Building at the corner was built in 1898 and
demolished in 1959 to make way for the United
Kingdom Building. Note the driving on the left;
Vancouver drivers switched to the right on
Jan. 1, 1922.

Firefly Books Ltd., 250 Sparks Ave., Willowdale, Ontario M2H 2S4

Permission of Vancouver Public Library

VANCOUVER *Flashbacks*

The Hollow Tree in Stanley Park, c. 1904. Tourists still like to pose in front of the tree for their photographs.

Firefly Books Ltd., 250 Sparks Ave., Willowdale, Ontario M2H 2S4

Permission of Vancouver Public Library

Carroll Street
Copyright applied for

VANCOUVER *Flashbacks*

Corner of Carrall and Water streets, May 1886. When
the sawmills opened in the 1860s, Gastown flourished
with its saloons, hotels and shops.

Firefly Books Ltd., 250 Sparks Ave., Willowdale, Ontario M2H 2S4

Permission of Vancouver Public Library

VANCOUVER *Flashbacks*

Looking south on Burrard from Hastings, 1931.
Construction began on the new Hotel Vancouver in
1928 and took until 1939 to complete.

Firefly Books Ltd., 250 Sparks Ave., Willowdale, Ontario M2H 2S4

Permission of Vancouver Public Library

HEADQUARTERS FOR KLONDIKE SUPPLIES.
DUNN & CO. Limited HARDWARE.
DUNN & CO. Limited HARDWARE.
DUNN & CO. Limited HARDWARE

VANCOUVER *Flashbacks*

Thomas Dunn & Co., hardware merchant, 8–10 Water, 1898. During the Klondike Gold Rush, shops did a booming business outfitting hopeful miners heading for the Yukon.

Firefly Books Ltd., 250 Sparks Ave., Willowdale, Ontario M2H 2S4

Permission of Vancouver Public Library

VANCOUVER *Flashbacks*

Lions Gate Bridge under construction, 1938. The
bridge was built by the Guinness family in order to
develop the British Properties, an exclusive
subdivision on the West Vancouver hillside.

Firefly Books Ltd., 250 Sparks Ave., Willowdale, Ontario M2H 2S4

Permission of Vancouver Public Library

VANCOUVER *Flashbacks*

English Bay, 1925. There is now a backdrop of high-rises, but English Bay is still a popular summer spot.

Firefly Books Ltd., 250 Sparks Ave., Willowdale, Ontario M2H 2S4

Permission of Vancouver Public Library

VANCOUVER *Flashbacks*

Southwest Hastings and Main, 1920. The building on the left served as City Hall 1896–1929. The Carnegie Library (right) is now a drop-in community centre, where there is still a library.

Firefly Books Ltd., 250 Sparks Ave., Willowdale, Ontario M2H 2S4

Permission of Vancouver Public Library

VANCOUVER *Flashbacks*

R. V. Winch Fruit and Game Store, 66 Cordova,
c. 1888.

Firefly Books Ltd., 250 Sparks Ave., Willowdale, Ontario M2H 2S4

Permission of Vancouver Public Library

VANCOUVER *Flashbacks*

Downtown Vancouver, looking over Coal Harbour,
1931. The Marine Building (centre) and the Georgia
Hotel (left foreground) are both surrounded today by
high office buildings.

Firefly Books Ltd., 250 Sparks Ave., Willowdale, Ontario M2H 2S4

Permission of Vancouver Public Library

VANCOUVER *Flashbacks*

J. W. Horne's real estate office, near Georgia and
Granville, 1886. With Vancouver soon to become the
terminus of the Canadian Pacific Railway, the new city
experienced a building boom.

Firefly Books Ltd., 250 Sparks Ave., Willowdale, Ontario M2H 2S4

Permission of Vancouver Public Library

VANCOUVER *Flashbacks*

Chinese street arch on Pender erected for Vancouver's
Golden Jubilee, 1936. Beginning to recover from the
worst of the Depression, Vancouver celebrated its
fiftieth birthday.

Firefly Books Ltd., 250 Sparks Ave., Willowdale, Ontario M2H 2S4

Permission of Vancouver Public Library

VANCOUVER *Flashbacks*

Capilano Suspension Bridge in North Vancouver, 1904. Suspended 230 feet above the creek bottom, this first suspension bridge was built of hemp cables in 1889.

Firefly Books Ltd., 250 Sparks Ave., Willowdale, Ontario M2H 2S4

Permission of Vancouver Public Library

VANCOUVER *Flashbacks*

West side of Carrall, Chinatown, c. 1906. Many Chinese workers came to British Columbia to construct the CPR. Although they faced strong prejudices, many settled in Vancouver and started businesses.

Firefly Books Ltd., 250 Sparks Ave., Willowdale, Ontario M2H 2S4

Permission of Vancouver Public Library

VANCOUVER *Flashbacks*

The CPR station at the foot of Granville, early 1900s.
The chateau-style station built in 1898 was replaced
by a larger station in 1914. *Princess Charlotte,* docked
at the wharf, provided passenger service along the
B.C. coast from 1909 to 1948.

Firefly Books Ltd., 250 Sparks Ave., Willowdale, Ontario M2H 2S4

Permission of Vancouver Public Library

VANCOUVER *Flashbacks*

A makeshift city hall after the fire of June 13, 1886.
Although the fire destroyed most of the townsite, the
city was quickly rebuilt.

Firefly Books Ltd., 250 Sparks Ave., Willowdale, Ontario M2H 2S4

Permission of Vancouver Public Library

VANCOUVER *Flashbacks*

Sailing ships loading lumber at Hastings Mill, c. 1906.
The sawmill at the foot of Dunlevy was a major
employer 1867–1930.

Firefly Books Ltd., 250 Sparks Ave., Willowdale, Ontario M2H 2S4

Permission of Vancouver Public Library

VANCOUVER *Flashbacks*

Looking north on Granville from Smythe, c. 1917. The
tall building on the left was an earlier Hotel
Vancouver. The Vancouver Block (right) still keeps
time with its 22-foot diameter clock.

Firefly Books Ltd., 250 Sparks Ave., Willowdale, Ontario M2H 2S4

Permission of Vancouver Public Library

VANCOUVER *Flashbacks*

Oxen hauling logs over a skid road near the foot of
Thurlow, 1882. Most of the timber was red cedar with
some Douglas fir.

Firefly Books Ltd., 250 Sparks Ave., Willowdale, Ontario M2H 2S4

Permission of Vancouver Public Library

First train in Vancouver

VANCOUVER *Flashbacks*

The arrival of the first CPR passenger train at Vancouver, May 23, 1887. Locomotive 374 was decorated with a photo of Queen Victoria and the words "Montreal Greets the Terminal City."

Firefly Books Ltd., 250 Sparks Ave., Willowdale, Ontario M2H 2S4

Permission of Vancouver Public Library

VANCOUVER *Flashbacks*

Looking west on Hastings from Cambie towards the Marine Building, 1935. This fine building, still admired today, was lavishly built in 1929-30 for $2.5 million.

Firefly Books Ltd., 250 Sparks Ave., Willowdale, Ontario M2H 2S4

Permission of Vancouver Public Library